50 ESSENTIAL TIPS TO GETTING AND KEEPING THE "RIGHT" JOB

STACEY YOUNG RIVERS

DEDICATION

This book is dedicated to my son. Your unconditional love and support means the world to me.

CONTENTS

ACKNOWLEDGMENTS

Thank you to my family and friends who have supported me through this effort:

- Grace Dyson, thank you for telling me to write.
- Careshia Moore, thank you for telling me to blog.
- Deborah Anderson-Singleton, thank you for giving me the puzzle pieces.

INTRODUCTION

---

50 Essential Tips To Getting and Keeping The "Right" Job is a compilation of simple ideas for effectively managing your career. Today, employees want to work in an engaging environment with opportunities for growth and advancement, and deciphering how to get there can be challenging. It is up to the individual to find the information and resources needed to navigate the challenges that come with obtaining a job or maintaining a solid performance level in the organization. While there is no one place to find all the answers for how to navigate career pitfalls, this book packages experience and expertise into tips that are simple and effective.

In this age of instant information, it's important for you to have access to knowledge that is useful, practical, impactful, and delivered in a concise manner. I affectionately call this book, "the list of fives" because each chapter provides 5 suggestions, for a total of 50 tips, for career planning. The book is divided into two sections: **Finding The Right Job**, and **Keeping The Right Job**, designed to quickly target your area of focus. The tips in each chapter can be used individually or collectively, but it is important to note that the "right"" job will be specific to your unique desires, and this will look different for each person.

Regardless of your career stage (entry level, intermediate, or experienced), your goal should be to first define what you want to accomplish, and then determine how you will get there. Enlisting the support of a career coach, mentor, or trusted friend is always helpful when making decisions that will affect the course of your career path. Getting and keeping the "right" job depends on your goals and plans, and this book will enhance your approach by outlining the essential tips to include in your strategy.

"Your destiny is on the horizon, how you get there is the beauty in the journey".

-Stacey Young Rivers

PART I

GETTING THE "RIGHT" JOB

1

WHAT YOU SHOULD KNOW ABOUT GETTING THE "RIGHT" JOB

Managing your career is not just about getting a job and performing the duties required for compensation, but also feeding your interests, utilizing your skills, and creating opportunities for growth and advancement. Before you can successfully find the right job, you must first know what you want if you will be effective in your search. **There are 10 key questions you should know about yourself:**

1. What are your skills?
2. What are you passionate about?
3. What is the salary range you are targeting?
4. Do you like to travel?
5. Are you willing to relocate?
6. Do you network? How broad is your list of connections?
7. What are your strengths and weaknesses?
8. Do you have a mentor? If not, why not?
9. Does your education level commensurate with the job you desire?
10. Who is performing in the role you want? Do you have access to them?

These questions all provide a starting point for some of the decisions you will make as you determine what is next for you. Building a plan to secure a role that you have very little information about can wreak havoc on your career. Understanding who you are and what motivates you will point you in the right direction for what will fulfill you in the long term.

In this section, you will read about ways to position yourself for getting the job you want. Once you answer the key questions, be prepared to build on those answers as you move through each chapter. Review the tips provided and assess if it feels directionally correct for where you want to go. I recommend that you discuss your thoughts with someone who can help guide you in your decision-making. Let's get started.

2

---

5 Tactics to Challenge Yourself Out of Mediocrity

I read an article in Atlanta Magazine that said Ted Turner learned to set goals he could not accomplish. Putting this statement into context from the article, Mr. Turner's intention was not about actually accomplishing his goals, but rather to not succumb because there was nothing left to aspire to. As a result, the empire he has built is evidence that setting lofty goals can challenge you to aim higher and accomplish more than you even believed possible.

While Ted is a modern day genius, that does not mean ordinary people like you and me can't learn from his successes. The challenge will be to determine *your* formula for success. Using lofty goals is a great way to push further and maybe even faster; the key is to find what works for you, and that will look very different for you, me, and Ted Turner.

There are 5 easy ways to get started on a new journey, propelling you closer to your goals:

1) **Gradually Add More** - A very practical approach to pursuing goals is to start small and build from there. For example, if it's your goal to be a project manager, application developer, etc., look at the basics of what it takes to get started and move forward. Anyone who is thriving in their job had to make

a start somewhere before they reached their goal. It takes one step at a time, and the key is to get started! Since we can be our own worst critic, you have to balance meeting the challenge with not being too critical that you will want to give up. Instead of quitting, make a pact with yourself to start fresh everyday and just keep going.

TIP: Determine what you can easily accomplish to get started. Make a list of simple tasks such as an informational interview to find out the details for what it will take to be successful in the career or role you have chosen. Once you have checked off every task on your simple list, make another list and continue the process. Although the tasks may start to get more challenging, keep a gauge on your progress and utilize an accountability partner to support you to complete your list.

2) Face Your Fears - False Evidence Appearing Real is a great description that demystifies fear and can make trying a new experience easier to comprehend. Most times people have fears because it represents the unknown or the worst thing we believe can happen. Fears can be small and large, but we all have them and the objective is not to allow it to paralyze you from moving forward. I had a fear of flying and knew I would never be able to experience more in life if I did not overcome it. While the fear was something that had no real cause, it was only "what if scenarios" that made me rationalize myself out of living life. I have a friend who tried sky-diving once because she wanted to face her fears and ended up with an out-of-this-world-encounter that she absolutely loved and will always treasure. The by-product of her experience made her bolder about other choices in her life, and since then, she has re-dedicated herself to projects that had been on the shelf for years.

TIP: Explore the specifics behind your fear - what frightens you and why. Talk with a career coach or mentor about your concerns to help you validate if the fear is a real concern or if you are just rationalizing yourself out of moving forward. Determine alternative options to eliminate fear from ruling your decisions. At the end of your life, what will matter most: your fears or your legacy?

3) Experiment To Learn - Who says you have to have all the answers before you begin? Turn this perception around by starting a business, standing up a website, publishing a book, or anything you want to know more about for the express purpose of learning. There is nothing like practical experience to bring clarity to your life. The objective is to give yourself permission to do it as a "student of life" without the pressure of succeeding or failing. Regardless of what it becomes, you will be wiser and better for having gone through the process.

TIP: To make this an enjoyable experience, pick something you like and will do for free. Just because you have to work does not mean it has to feel like work. Keep a journal or blog of what you are learning and share your new found knowledge with others who may need encouragement and find it useful.

4) Start A Collaboration Group - As the saying goes, "birds of a feather flock together", and this is true for like-minded individuals. I get fuel from being in the company of people who are passionate, progressive, living life on purpose, and daring to fulfill their dreams. What energizes you? Seek out those people and meet regularly to catch up, get and give consultation, and even barter services. You'll find that chasing after your goals is so much easier in the company of people who support and inspire you to keep going.

TIP: Collaboration can begin with two people, and instead of trying to sync the schedule of a group, start small, and then add more. Set a regular date and time so you can invite others. The purpose is to build support for your professional or personal projects while getting advice, information, and even introduced to connections who can help you on your journey.

5) Volunteer Your Services - One of the best and easiest ways to gain experience, develop skills, and help others in the process is by volunteering your time and talents to a cause. Become the lead for your alumni organization, home owner association, charitable organization, small church group, or any other role that will develop your skills in leadership, finance, marketing, communication, etc. Volunteering is always a bi-directional benefit, you help others while helping yourself to develop in areas that are transferrable.

TIP: Know your bandwidth, start small, then build on what you can handle. Volunteering is one of the easiest ways to damage your reputation if you can't manage the load that you are being given. Always communicate your availability or what you can reasonably accomplish.

3

THE 5 P's TO CAREER PERFECTION

We all have choices to make in our careers and while you may not be able to change anything about the past, you can be purposeful and intentional going forward. Acknowledging that you are the owner of your career and responsible for the successes and failures you experience is the first step to creating the career you want. It would be great if creating a successful career was as easy as going to the salad bar, choosing what you like, and leaving the rest. The harsh reality is, it takes **people, planning, performance, progress,** and **persistence** to achieve a career that is perfect for you. Defining success for yourself sets the stage for the decisions you must make and the best time to start is now.

Why do you need to know this? Career Management can be stressful, and having an understanding of 5 key areas can simplify your focus and give you a clear outlook for your decisions.

1) People - Who do you know that can help with where you are trying to go? I learned early in my career that people are willing to help if: **A) You know what you want, and B) You have the courage to ask.**

Assistance can come in the form of feedback, job leads, introductions, mentoring, coaching, informational interviews, etc. You will need a myriad of expertise at your finger tips based on the different challenges you may encounter, so make sure your digital rolodex is broad enough to give you an eclectic list from which to choose. **Offer to help others, so when you need to ask for help, it is a reciprocal process.**

2) Planning - In project management, the term "progressive elaboration" is a project manager's best friend. No one can possibly know everything there is to know from the start of anything, so planning is something that should happen frequently. The very nature of a plan is to determine what you want to manifest and how to get there, but exactly what will happen along the way is a mystery. What you can do to exude some control over your plan is determine what you want, take ownership for achieving your action items, adjust as needed, and mitigate your risks for any setbacks that may occur. **Outline your plan today, and as you get clarity about your direction, then make your plan more definitive.**

3) Performance - Your performance is your calling card - perform well and people will know who you are. Some people can be misled that if they are looking for another job, it doesn't matter if they are performing poorly in the one they currently have. This is wrong thinking and damaging to your brand. Just as people know when you are performing well, they also know when you are a poor performer. It's always best to do your best and leave on a good note with references.

4) Progress - Progress is valuable in any area but it's only impactful and fulfilling when you are advancing in the area you want to be in. For example, becoming a nurse is a great accomplishment but if that is not where you see yourself in 5 years or more, then how will you continue to make progress? And if you should make progress, will it be enjoyable? By first determining where you see yourself in the future and taking small steps to get there, you can make progress towards something that will benefit you professionally and personally.

5) Persistence - Failure can only occur when you decide to give up, and this is where persistence can set you apart from everyone else, period. While I was still in college working towards my bachelor's degree, I met a woman who had just obtained her PhD. I admired her discipline and asked how did she get through it. She didn't give a lot of details, but what she did say was very compelling. She said, "It took me 10 years to complete my PhD and I realized that 10 years was going to pass regardless so I might as well have my degree at the end ". **The time will pass anyway, where will you be at the end?**

I don't advise "luck" as a career strategy, you have to be intentional and prepared. Some of us can get lucky by being in the right place at the right time, but learning how to sustain and progress will become the next problem to solve. I believe that success is attained through a conscious effort to take action on our heart's desire. By planning, preparing, performing well, connecting with people, and being persistent, you create the thing you say you want, and if you start now, you will be one day closer to achieving your goal.

4

5 Ways to Keep Your Skills Sharp

How people obtain an education today is no longer one size fits all. Colleges and universities continue to strategize about how to diversify their offerings to keep in step with consumers and technology. Since the way in which you choose to consume information and develop your skills is personal to you, the challenge then becomes how to keep your skills sharp. I have found the best way to stay in the game is to be open to different ways of sharpening your existing skills and creative about how you develop new skills.

Here are five ways to give your skills a workout to remain relevant:

1) INTERVIEWS

Applying for a job can be stressful but not being prepared for what to wear, what to say, or how to make a positive impression, will put a damper on anyone's chances for actually getting hired. Preparing for an interview will make you fine-tune your wardrobe, resume, and presentation skills. Ask trusted colleagues who are versed in the interviewing and hiring process to **participate in a mock interview** with you to provide immediate feedback. If you have access to executives who are willing to help in this area, this can arm you with a different perspective about your brand. Not only will you find out how well you performed, but also how sought after your skills are on your resume. Periodically scheduling mock interviews will give you the opportunity to work through the details of the interview process, and a little research will help you determine your value in the industry.

2) CERTIFICATION

In today's job market, differentiating yourself from the rest may take a little time and money. One of the smartest ways to stand out and say that you are serious about your career is to **gain a certification** in your field. A certification illustrates that you are committed to your career and value the expertise needed to excel. If your employer sponsors your certification, this is a tremendous perk. If not, don't wait until you are asked, take the initiative and invest your time and money into your future. Research your area of interest and ensure you understand the requirements to maintain the certification. Join a professional organization to engage with others and stay abreast of trends.

3) MASSIVE OPEN ONLINE COURSES

With the proliferation of technology comes opportunities to engage consumers in a way that disrupts the traditional means of use. One of those areas is higher education, and with the accessibility of information via the internet, colleges have been making their course content available for free, drawing an interest in topics that range from finance to creative writing. While their reasoning for doing this may vary, the benefit to you is the ability to **audit a course at MIT, Harvard, or Yale and get the latest trend on the academia thought process**. Browse some of the free online courses to see if any fit your expectations. If not, you can always audit any college course for a price if you are not seeking a degree.

4) FREELANCING

Working for yourself takes a certain drive, discipline, and organization, and although you may not want to be CEO of your own company, you can **be CEO of your own schedule by freelancing your skills**. This is a great way to build references, recommendations, and a professional network of colleagues who can provide leads and information for new jobs and unique projects. Freelancing is also an outlet for developing new skills you may not get to use in your day job. The great benefit of this tactic is the ability to move on to a new opportunity if the current one isn't meeting your expectations.

5) VOLUNTEERING

Some people may describe volunteering as "working for free" because there is not a monetary payment for your services, however, there is a form of payment that can be more valuable than money. Think about it this way, money comes and goes, but **skills amassed through volunteering stays with you for a lifetime and gives you the ability to earn (more) money.** There are many organizations looking for help, and while some may want your resume before they will appoint you to certain positions, there are many more who welcome the fact that someone is willing to give their time and talent to furthering their mission. I do think it's important that whatever organization you decide to give your time to represents something that you are passionate about or at least have a strong interest in. This factor alone will make a big difference in what feels like work or purpose

5

THE TOP 5 TIPS FOR FINDING THE "RIGHT" JOB

If you are looking for your next job opportunity, then it is very timely that you are reading this book. The takeaway for you will be to translate this advice into practical wisdom to find the right job. Before you change your approach, it's imperative that you are sure about what you want directionally from your career. Knowing what you want now and in the future is the groundwork on which you will make your choices. Being confident about this foundation empowers you to move forward without hesitation. In addition, defining what "winning" means to you gives you a criteria for success that any employment offer can be judged against. Consider having more depth for your decision-making than just receiving a job proposition, but one which also leverages your skills and the opportunity to grow your career.

Take a moment and review the questions below.

Think about how you would answer if interviewed today.

- Who are you? (Tell me about yourself)
- What are your skills and expertise?
- When have you been passionate about your work?

- Why do you want to work for Company X?
- How will you support the company/department in its goals?
- Do you have any questions?

CHANGE YOUR PERSPECTIVE

All interviewers ask the general questions listed above at some point during the process. Having a solid understanding of your career goals can change your perspective for the interview and place you on a level playing field with the recruiter and hiring manager. Knowing your career plan will minimize doubt for how to answer questions as well as what information will be important to extract during the exchange. **You should be able to make an informed decision about whether this is the right situation for you, not if your answers are what interviewers want to hear.**

THE INTERVIEW DEFINED

An interview, at the very essence, is a conversation between you and your potential employer. It is a reciprocation of information that may culminate into a partnership agreement. You should know your strengths and weaknesses, what you want and don't want in your next job, and prepared to ask the strategic questions during the interview that will aid in your decision to accept the offer. The "agreement" is only a success when both parties are transparent and forthcoming with the information each need to know. **At the end of the day, it is absolutely okay to graciously decline any offer that will not meet your needs.**

Of all the articles you have read and all the advice you have been given, let's focus on 5 essential tips that will take the headache out of preparing for your next interview. Remember, this approach is effective when you are building upon a solid plan for your career.

Determine what resonates with you from this list and discover how you can enhance your interview approach.

1) Personal Board of Directors - Create a circle of your colleagues who you trust and utilize their expertise to help build your plan. From creating the perfect interview packet to providing feedback using a mock interview format, your circle of experts should support you in your goal to be polished and presentable. Contact your personal board with as much lead time as possible to engage them in your plan.

2) Resume - I have read hundreds of resumes and found that creating an effective resume is more challenging than you think. Contrary to popular belief, this information is not just for providing your work history, rather it is an extension of you and your capabilities. The key is to write and organize the details in a way that will capture a recruiter or hiring manager's attention. Other than your work experience, important sections such as the objective, skills, accomplishments, and community service all tell if you are a potential fit. Investing in a professional resume service can be worth the price if you need help and want something that really illustrates who you are. Review your profile and make sure the message is positive and it's congruent across all social platforms. What you have in your LinkedIn profile should translate to your resume. Google yourself and know what is discoverable, mitigating the opportunity to be surprised by what you can be asked about.

3) Attire - Have you heard the advice, "dress for the role you want, not the job you have today"? This can be applied in a few different ways, but let's be practical about what is feasible and reasonable for you. A great percentage of the interview process is to determine if you are a match for the role (skills and culture). "Fitting in" should be important for you as it is for the hiring manager.

Connect with those who can give you insight into the company's culture and couture. If you don't want to wear a tie everyday, why apply for a position where a tie is required?

4) Research - Know as much as you can about the company you are targeting. Finding out who they are and the actions they have taken can be as simple as a Google search. From a finance perspective, if it is a publicly traded company, access filings to understand their fiscal health. Arm yourself with info about who you may be going to work for and draw out the hard to find nuggets from your interviewer with questions about the company. Never come to an interview empty handed. At a minimum, have a copy of your resume and any samples of your work. Based on your field, work samples will look different for everyone, so think of it as a tangible example of your best work. For strategic or executive roles, highlighting ways to address challenges in the area you are interviewing for can showcase your expertise. Gauging the questions asked or reaction to your work samples can give you insight into what performance expectations may be once hired.

5) Mock Interview - As mentioned in the previous chapter, the mock interview is an invaluable tool to help you prepare for the real thing. If possible, use colleagues who have experience interviewing to walk through the process with you. The session should be as realistic as possible, but the bonus is you get immediate feedback about anything that could derail your interview. Everything from eye contact, attitude, nervous behaviors, and the quality of your answers should all be observed to give you insight into where you can improve.

6

5 Clever Ways to Upgrade Your Job Search

Searching for a job has significantly changed in recent years. Some of us remember when the only way to find out what jobs were available was to check the classifieds section of the local newspaper. Sites like Monster, Indeed, Simply Hired, Zip Recruiter, and The Ladders all provide great leads, but LinkedIn proved to be the game changer by providing a social aspect to the job search. Prior to 2003 when LinkedIn launched, who knew that it would have been possible to virtually network while looking for job prospects at the same time? If you are a job seeker, one of the most important things you can do is create an effective profile, and that goes well beyond LinkedIn.

When thinking about how to improve your job search, you may conjure up an image of a huge, complicated process that can drain your time and energy to find the perfect solution. Not so. Developing a personalized formula can make the simple things significant when blended in a way that takes the ordinary to the next level. This is not as difficult as you might think, it just takes starting small and being consistent.

Begin by assessing how you can change your game to redefine your process. With technology and a little creativity, you can create your own formula for getting recruiters to call back.

Here are suggestions to seed you with ideas for finding your next opportunity:

1) Stand Up Your Own Website or Blog - Illustrate who you are by creating content and posting it on your own site. Uniquely designing your resume, blogging about a topic of interest, creating videos, sharing your photography portfolio, etc. all allow you to showcase your talent in a way that is tangible and more impactful than trying to sell yourself in a cover letter alone.

2) Create a Network of Recruiters - Fast track your resume by sharing that you are available for offers with a network of recruiters. The challenge recruiters have is finding the right person, for the right job, with the right skills, at the right time. Help them help you by making it easy to be found, documenting your resume in a way that makes your skills (including transferable skills) and experience easily accessible. Connect on LinkedIn, at job fairs, through colleagues, etc. The best time to create your network is when you are not pressed for a job.

3) Launch Your Video Resume - Showcasing your personality on video can be a risky option but may also pay off big. Hiring managers are looking for talent who not only have the expertise to do the job, but also the visible aspects that will mesh well with the team and culture. Have you ever been told you were not a fit? This has a lot to do with personality, which is very important in getting work done and accomplishing goals. If you feel you have a great personality and will meld with any culture, then a video resume can give you an edge over others by advertising what a great hire you are.

4) Teach An Online Course - Showcase your skills and take it to the next level by teaching a course online. Massive Open Online Courses are fast becoming one of the largest online learning centers that gives you the ability to develop your brand in a new way by using this platform and your expertise. You can offer your services for free or a set a price to share your knowledge.

Gain credibility from your students through course ratings and evaluations. Once your course is available, use it on your resume to market yourself in your chosen subject.

5) Engage Your Network - Eliminate the hassle of looking for business cards by connecting via LinkedIn at an event. Once your invite is accepted, send a personalized "thank you" message and leave an open invitation for coffee, lunch, or even a "coffee call" if not local. Whether you are immediately taken up on your offer or not, you have set the stage for a response and a possible new business relationship.

Important: Don't forget to be authentic in every transaction and think about how you can reciprocate any help you are given. The goal is to find an opportunity, not come across as opportunistic.

Creating an effective job search strategy includes honing your brand AND your approach to landing the role you desire. **Upgrade your job search by showcasing your capabilities outside of the standard documented resume.** Engage others by making impactful changes to the way you communicate who you are. Your willingness to make small changes may culminate into something big, or innovative, that is rewarding.

7

5 KEY STEPS TO STANDING OUT

Competitive Advantage is described as providing great value through differentiation resulting from matching core competencies to opportunities. It is the extraordinary in an ordinary world that gets the attention of those looking for something new and useful. In some people we immediately see their competitive advantage, and while this specific formula works for them, trying to copy their formula will not work for you for a myriad of reasons. At the essence of this dilemma is the challenge of figuring out what is unique about you.

This is not a vain, ego-centric exercise, but rather an honest, objective view of who you are and what you do well. To validate what you think your strengths are may take a professional assessment or confirmation from people who know you well and will be honest with their feedback. Your goal is to find **your** formula that you can harness, develop, and make your brand. The opportunity is locating where your "brand" is useful and valuable, then leveraging it in a way that engages others.

This is not an overnight exercise, and not impossible either. If you desire to carve out a niche for yourself, then there is a starting place where you can begin this process:

1) **Assess your strengths** - Identify your strengths by determining what you do well <u>and</u> enjoy. Build on your strengths by gaining expertise in an area that complements what you already do well. For instance, if one of your

strengths is being a natural communicator, then attend Toastmasters sessions and gain a Distinguished Toastmaster certification.

By taking what you do naturally and adding a level of credibility, people will seriously engage with you because of this.

2) **Develop a strategy for how to leverage your skills** - Once you add a level of credibility to your strength(s), assess how you will leverage your skills to build your brand. Don't worry if you don't have a complete plan or know exactly how this will play out. Take the first step and build as you go. Give yourself permission to change course as needed, but continue to work towards your goal.

3) **Find supporters** - We all need supportive people in our corner to encourage and assist at times. Find those who will give you the kind of honesty you need to be your best self <u>and</u> will keep your information confidential.

4) **Take calculated risks and stretch assignments** - Put your self to the test by trying new assignments and taking risks that will make you better for having gone through it. Outline the risks and how to mitigate them before going forward.

5) **Examine re-inventing yourself** - It's important to be self-aware and understand if you have created an image that is not perceived well. This is a process in which you will have to be ready to hear the hard feedback. Until you do this, you may not be able to make the progress and impact you desire.

Be consistent and have patience if your progress does not happen as quickly as you would like. Remember, you are uniquely and wonderfully made, and while the journey may not yield immediate results, you must stay the course if you will find your competitive advantage. It's important to find time to work on you as a project, setting goals and milestones. You should periodically review your accomplishments and strategically look at how you move forward. If you want a more fulfilling career, aren't you worth the time and effort?

PART II

KEEPING THE "RIGHT" JOB

8

WHAT YOU NEED TO KNOW ABOUT KEEPING THE "RIGHT" JOB

Companies are constantly looking for the right talent and this can be especially challenging if the role is specialized. To stay in the game you must remain relevant by keeping your skills current or by gaining experience in a new area. This may mean investing in yourself if the company does not offer the specific training you want. Gaining new skills is a value add to your resume while adding value to your brand. Besides having the right skills, cultivating relationships are important for sharing opportunities and building influence. At the end of the day, it is about delivering results and helping others in the process. Use these key suggestions to create a career plan to keep the right job, and position yourself for the next one.

1. Manage your career like a business - stay competitive and create strategic goals.
2. Ensure you stay current on skills and trends in your industry - this will allow you to be on the forefront of changes as the business moves forward.
3. Garner visibility by taking stretch assignments or volunteering to take on more responsibility.

4. Network outside of your organization and build valuable relationships that will make you resourceful.
5. Understand the company's overall strategy and goals to ensure you are aligned with where it is headed.

This section of the book is about taking accountability for your performance and balancing it with your manager's expectations. Most times, employees don't consider two very important aspects of gainful employment: Staying relevant and planning for the future, which are primary key components of career management. Employees, not managers, are accountable for their careers and the state that it is in, good or bad. Managers have the huge challenge of ensuring quality of work, alignment with the company's strategies, compliance with policies, and managing their own careers. Helping employees understand their performance level, partnering for development plans, and supporting training needs are also part of a manager's role, but don't be mistaken that training is career management. If you haven't been taking ownership for your career, start today. Read the following chapters and identify a plan to move your career forward.

9

5 Easy Techniques to Give Your Manager Feedback

The performance review season is a great time to level set, close out the old and start with the new. Even if you were a rock star last year and over-achieved on your goals, it starts all over and the company is now asking "What have you done for me lately?", (a throwback to the Janet Jackson 80's tune). **You may need more from your manager this year if you will effectively deliver on goals, and this is when knowing how to give feedback can aid in your success.** Giving feedback can be a touchy subject because there is a right and wrong way, and if not given correctly, you are taking a huge risk that may damage relationships. If you are contemplating sharing your concerns, here are some things to consider before you get started.

So how do you give your manager feedback? Review the questions below BEFORE you walk into his office and share your thoughts about his management style.

- Have you been trained to give and receive feedback?
- How will your feedback impact the relationship?
- Is the feedback specific to you or the entire team?
- Are you the right person to deliver the feedback?

- Is your manager having personal or career challenges?
- Is this the right time given the circumstances?
- Do you avoid pointing fingers at others?
- What is your motivation for giving the feedback?
- Do you have expectations that something will change?
- If the situation does not improve, can you manage through it?

These questions may help you determine what can go well as a result of your courage, or horribly wrong and cause more damage than you anticipated. Being honest with yourself will help you to make the right decisions about your go-forward plan. Talk with a mentor or career coach about your questions to make sure your approach is correct. **If you are not discouraged and still want to give your manager feedback, here are some tips for getting started.**

1) **Establish a Working Relationship** - Do you have a working relationship or is he just the person that gives you your assignment for the day? Some people are uncomfortable with talking about anything other than work, but since we are all people, there's more to us than just work. Figure out how to casually ask how was his weekend, if he's wearing new glasses, did he change the feng shui in his office, anything outside of the assignment but not too personal. The goal is to develop a casual conversation that will allow you both to gain a level of comfort with each other. Constructive feedback will be received through a positive lens when there is a rapport established.

2) **Give Him Kudos** - Another way to establish a rapport is to tell people what you genuinely value about them. Giving positive feedback is a great way to bring balance to the relationship. Have you given him positive feedback lately? Did you tell him what a great job he did with the Supply & Demand Report? Or the team presentation he delivered a week ago that gave you more insight into the purpose for the product? Managers are rarely given a pat on the back, and the higher you move up in the organization, the

kudos become less because you are expected to deliver. Be sincere and always try to give genuine praise before finding fault or sharing the "what's wrong now" report.

3) **Ask For Feedback**- This is a tactic that can open the door for you to request what you need to be effective. Consider this role play to illustrate the point:

(Role Play This Scenario With A Trusted Colleague):

You knock on his door and ask if he has a few minutes. He says "Yes, come in". You make small talk for a minute or two (but not longer). You change the topic to talk about the assignment that you are currently working on and the challenge you're encountering. It's important to focus on the process and not the people, if possible. Most times employees are blamed for a bad process that they had nothing to do with creating. When he tells you what you should do to overcome the challenge, you say, "May I ask something of you as well?" (here comes your request). He'll look at you intrigued and say, "Yes of course". You say (respectfully), "Can you change your message to the team? It seems that people have misunderstood and now we are going down the wrong path". What comes next should be a candid conversation about the problem and potential solutions. The goal is to make him understand how he can help resolve the problem. Blaming others is counter-productive and does not portray you as a leader – delivering results will. This takes courage and humility, but should be a start in the right direction.

4) **Offer Your Help** - How do you acquire more work when you are trying to resolve an issue? Because you care enough to bring the concern to your manager's attention, and this will set you apart from everyone else. Offering your help says you are not the bearer of bad news, but solution-oriented and committed to seeing it through to resolution. Employees who are adept at problem-solving are what every manager wants on their team.

5) **Always Check Your Motivation and Your Facts** - The last thing you want is to be blind-sided by his response to your feedback. Make sure you ask questions and gather objective information for why something happened the way it did. In my experience, I have found that the issue was not intentional and there were other reasons outside of my manager's control for why certain things occurred. It's important to have a relationship where you feel comfortable giving your manager feedback, and while you are working there, you might as well invest in creating an environment worth coming to everyday.

10

5 Ways to Challenge Your Boss for a Better Performance Review

Managing people is a skill that does not come easily, especially for new managers. Most people are promoted to managing a team because they excelled at the technical or hard skills, which is just one of the job requirements. The role of manager also requires the soft skills, which are equally important for connecting with and motivating employees to perform. While these skills may be lacking in some, a manager's deficiency in soft or hard skills does not negate the responsibility you have for your own performance. Although some employees believe that career development is their manager's responsibility, the reality is, your performance is the foundation of YOUR career. **You have to learn how to advocate for yourself to get the best possible results, and to accomplish this, you must engage your manager to address your performance needs.** These suggestions can't take the place of solid performance, however, if you want to take strategic steps to improve, here are some ideas to get you started:

1) **Initiate a job performance conversation.** If your manager does not schedule performance meetings, then you should schedule a conversation. Find out her availability and send an agenda in advance for a productive exchange. Get her buy-in to periodically schedule one-on-one sessions. Make sure you take notes and follow up in email so she can clarify anything that

you may have heard incorrectly. For some, this tactic alone may address the age old problem of hearing negative feedback for the first time during the review.

2) **Ask for feedback and utilize it to make improvements.** When asking for feedback make sure you are ready to accept what you will hear. Receiving constructive criticism can be difficult, especially if you are hearing it for the first time. Be diplomatic (not disagreeable), ask for specific examples, and committed to taking action on how you will improve.

This tactic can backfire if :

1. **You are not expecting to hear that you are failing in certain areas.**
2. **You neglect to take action on the feedback you have been given.**

Even if you disagree with what you have been told, you have to change the perception. While we all want to be a rock star at work, everyone has room for improvement, so seriously consider what is being shared. Asking for the hard feedback is a great way to let your manager know you want to advance. Listening to her constructive insight and using it to enhance your performance for the better gives you a greater chance to overachieve.

3) **Find out a problem that he is trying to solve and take it off his plate.** Everyone loves help at work, especially if it's a nagging problem that someone else resolves. Help your manager to help you by taking an issue off his list of things to do. This sets you up to score points for your initiative, leadership, and problem solving skills. Make sure that you resolve the issue or this could go in the opposite direction than what you had planned.

4) **Gain insight from your boss' boss.** Most times when decisions are made in the organization, they are made at higher levels to support the company's strategy. It's important for senior leaders to know who you are and the capabilities you possess.

If your organization does not encourage skip-level meetings, then meet with your boss first and let her know your plan to get to know your management team. While this conversation should eliminate any concerns of what your meeting will be about, for some, can still elicit apprehension about your motivation. If you feel this may be the case BEFORE you tell her, engage a mentor or career coach to strategize about how you can overcome this obstacle. Going around her can exacerbate the situation and make your relationship tense. At the end of the day, having a relationship with the senior leaders in your organization is helpful in providing insight for how you manage your career.

5) **Learn new skills and translate them into tangible results.** Learning a new skill is only valuable when you can use it to deliver results, personally or professionally. If you have learned a new skill recently, then you should demonstrate it in a way that shows tangible progress your manager can observe. Ask for a new responsibility, collaborate with peers to solve an issue, coach your boss on a process, or any activity allowing you to illustrate that you can effectively leverage your newly found knowledge. Document your experiences/accomplishments, including your peers' feedback for how you performed and where you can improve.

Employees who keep detailed notes about their performance during the year have a better chance at gaining a balance for what is written about them. Never skip an opportunity to document your self-review or talk about your accomplishments for the year. Challenging your boss takes courage and competency, but the overall benefit is for the health of your career.

11

5 THINGS TO DO WHEN YOUR MANAGER RESIGNS

When your manager quits, voluntary or not, what do you do? On the surface this may not sound like a problem or even an issue that needs addressing, but for those who understand there is a holistic approach to career management, there is a factor to especially consider after the departure of your immediate manager: Your leadership independence. If you have not been given visibility or support to effectively lead in the organization, there may be a gap between perception and reality concerning your leadership independence from the person you immediately reported to. The only way to minimize or eliminate this concern is by demonstrating your leadership in action and fostering relationships across the organization. If you have not had the opportunity to do this, there is still a strategy you can employ to remedy what others may incorrectly think about your abilities and potential.

There are generally three mistakes employees make that may contribute to their inability to navigate the organization in the wake of a manager's departure:

A) They have not been cultivating relationships across the organization.
B) They have been "Head Down Working", meaning, doing the work but not taking time to foster the other parts of their career in a holistic approach.
C) Their leadership independence have not been established.

Most times, employees are not aware of these subtleties which may detract from their ability to demonstrate their potential. When your manager leaves, you must take extra care to ensure that you are showing your value and building your brand. Your inability to dispel perceived loyalty to your former manager could skew the perception of your diplomacy. **Enhancing your performance, brand, relationships, and expertise is your job in totality, not just the function of delivering a product or service. When you have a holistic approach to your career, you will enhance your performance on purpose because you understand the interdependence of each of these areas.**

1) **Perform Well** - This goes without saying, you have to perform well in the job for which you are being paid. Some employees focus on the other areas of career management (training classes, networking, etc.) while their performance suffers. Great performance is the foundation of any role and ultimately creates your reputation.

2) **Create Allies** - Despite the department you reside in, it's imperative that you connect and collaborate with people across the organization. Even more, if there are ways to enhance your work product or service, this is a great way to showcase your diplomacy and understand the perspective or problem as a business case. Finding ways to effectively collaborate for positive results across teams can singularly do wonders for your brand.

3) **Showcase Your Expertise** - If you consider yourself to be an expert in a given area, how are you using this information to bring business value and enhance your brand? No one knows what you know unless you demonstrate your ability and potential. Performing as expected does not impress anyone, however demonstrating a persistent behavior to exceed the standard is what will garner everyone's attention.

Showcasing your expertise involves preparation, consistency, and going above and beyond the norm. Once you know your standard, figure out how you can bring it up a level or two. Become the "go to" person for the subject matter. Now is the time to strategize how you can enhance your brand to incorporate your expertise.

4) **Volunteer** - Using volunteering as a strategy to build your skills can be a great thing, or it can go horribly wrong if you are not careful. Make sure you communicate your bandwidth and follow through on anything you have committed to deliver. The strategic goal should be to expand your network and showcase your skills outside of your current role.

5) **Demonstrate Your Leadership** - It is imperative that you demonstrate your leadership skills, preferably while you are working under your manager's care. When decisions are made in the organization, it helps a great deal if people know your capabilities, especially senior leaders. Having a one-on-one session at least once or twice a year with your executive leader will help you gain insight into where the organization may be headed. This is input for your career plan to remain relevant in a changing environment.

12

5 Quick Points For Managing Change

Change is inevitable and the only constant you should allow yourself to grow comfortable with. While our human nature is to avoid change at all costs, change can present options when you are engaged and prepared. The key to managing change is to be realistic, have various sources from which to gather information, seek to understand the business drivers, and create a plan to give yourself the power of choice.

1) Google Alerts - One simple tactic you can use to stay abreast of the latest news in your industry is to create Google Alerts. Get an email delivered right to your in box when Google finds results that matches your search term. You can get the latest news about a company, product, or news story - even find out what might be said about you! Get information as soon as it is published on the web, discovering information not in the mainstream.

2) Key Relationships - Cultivating relationships with peers across the company can aid in understanding how changes are being implemented in different areas of the business. While some changes may or may not affect you directly, understanding generally what they are and why can help you unpack the business demands for change. Functional areas such as Finance, Legal, and HR are key areas in driving business strategies and will regularly adjust to support company goals. Having key relationships in these areas can aid in understanding certain decisions. Most of the time, companies will provide information about strategic changes, and there is one simple rule employees should always follow: Read all emails and talk with your manager about anything you don't understand.

3) **Professional Organizations** - A great way to build a network in your industry is by joining a professional organization. Having contacts at other companies can give you a broader reach outside of your organization and provide insight into changes happening in the industry. Find a professional group that aligns with your interests. To build effective relationships, support the organization when you can through your time and talents. Creating visibility in this area can be strategic and helpful when trying to navigate the pros and cons of change.

4) **Skills Management** - Understanding the importance of skills and how staying current or ahead of the curve can make you a valuable asset to the company, which is key to being employable. Make it a point to take inventory of your skills yearly and determine what you will enhance or add to your toolbox. Choose wisely and research the yields for what the specific skill will allow you to accomplish.

5) **Career Planning** - Aside from any changes that may be implemented in your company, career management should always be a personal priority. Generally, employees wait for managers to discuss career goals, help decide training needs, and outline performance expectations. This is something you can and should do for yourself. It's important to have a plan for what you want to do next and an outline for the path to get there. In most cases, you will need experience, training, or both, and the only way to obtain it is to plan ahead and look for prospects that are congruent with your goals.

Being proactive about acquiring information, managing relationships, and making your career a priority can take you from fearful to fearless when it comes to change. As a matter of fact, when you are in this mode, you will welcome change because it spells "opportunity".

13

5 Truths Nobody Tells You Before a Layoff

How do you manage through ambiguous times such as a restructure or lay-off? This is the question lots of employees ask during a season of change. While there is not a panacea for how to achieve this, I interviewed several executives who shared their insight. What they revealed begins well before a layoff and right up to getting the notice. The importance lies in the human view that we all share. Check out the tips below and take advantage of this wisdom to gain clarity for a situation you might be facing.

NEW LEADERSHIP

Employees should be aware of the "invisible change" that takes place in the organization. These are the unwritten rules that are never explicitly stated but understood. As with the inauguration of a new president, new leadership brings those invisible changes that you have to be aware of if you will continue to make the right decisions and meet expectations. **1) Try to gain a quick understanding of the new performance goals and always have "go to" people who can shed light on organizational changes.**

NEW FINANCIAL GOALS

The sole purpose for any for-profit organization is to make a profit. From time to time, companies will review financial strategies and make changes to increase productivity or decrease expenses to improve the bottom line. Always look for how you can stay connected to those changes.

If your role is not in an area that responsible for revenue generation, then utilize Lean Six Sigma to solve problems for the company. **2) Making proposals for improving the operation can go a long way to ensuring your department's success.** Track your accomplishments and create a portfolio of your work.

SHIFT IN COMPANY DIRECTION
I attended a seminar once where an employee asked an Executive Vice President if he could publish an email informing the organization every time the company made a change, entered into an agreement, or embarked on a new partnership. The EVP replied that it was impossible to do simply because HE did not always know. **3) One way to keep a pulse on your company is to subscribe to daily industry briefs to see what is transpiring at a macro-level in your world.** Most times you will get a glimpse of what changes are happening and even trends that may later impact your company.

ORGANIZATION RESTRUCTURE
Company-wide or not, changes are strategic for structuring the organization to provide the needed results. Whatever the reason, there is always uncertainty and a shift in morale that can impact perception and performance. If you are a manager, this is when the leader in you needs to truly lead. Bring as much consistency to your team as you can. When employees don't get information, they will find a way to get it, even if it's not the truth. **4) Share organizational changes with your team, including those that are indirect impacts, and deliver the information in a way employees can understand.** It may be difficult to grasp, but a restructure **is not** about you, it's about business. Organizational changes have a way of making you re-assess what you need out of your career, and your career **is** your business.

DOWNSIZING OR RIGHTSIZING

This is always the most challenging situation to manage through. There is no easy way to tell a person their services are no longer needed. **5) If you are a manager and have to deliver a severance notice, be sensitive and conduct the conversation in the way you would want someone to provide it to you.** If possible, allow employees to say their good-byes and gather their belongings. In some cases, you may have to do it for them. Whatever the situation may be, remember that you could see these same people again under a different circumstance and you should want that meeting to be as amicable as possible.

At the end of the day you may not be able to avoid a layoff, however if you have been managing your career like a business, then you should have options for what is next for you.

Remember to keep your values intact and let your good character illustrate who you are when times get tough. This is a sign that you will surely survive any season of change as well as gain a new respect that can't be bought.

14

NOT THE END, BUT THE BEGINNING

Your career is a journey that ends when you say it does and not a moment sooner. For those of us who have been on this journey for a while, as you look back and see the milestones and chapters you have created, it is possible to know that you can overcome anything. If you are just entering the workforce, have a plan and the patience to accomplish the goals you set for yourself. Anytime you are facing a concern, issue, or problem, you may not realize then that this is just a moment in time, and all you will have at the end is how you performed during this particular time in your life.

Instead of reacting in the moment:

1. Strive to understand your purpose
2. Make decisions with good intentions
3. Have expectations to make life better for you and those around you

This may be the end of the book but it can be the beginning of a new chapter for you. Set lofty goals and take it one day at a time. When it is truly the end, you will be glad that you invested in yourself and made work meaningful.

STACEY YOUNG RIVERS

If you want more practical advice for managing your career, look for my next book, "How To Get R.I.C.H. and Other Career Hacks". Join me on StaceyRivers.com to access new content to strategically manage your career

About the Author

Stacey Young Rivers is a strategic project leader and an avid blogger who loves to write about the career journey. She has a Bachelor's Degree in Technology Management and a Master's Degree in Management with a focus on Leadership & Organizational Effectiveness. She is a certified Human Capital Strategist and Strategic Workforce Planner by the Human Capital Institute. Rivers has been in the media industry for over 10 years and has achieved several awards including Technology Rising Star and Modern Day Technology Leader by the Career Communications Group, Inc. Rivers was awarded the Distinguished Alumni Award by her Alma Mater Clayton State University, and has served on several boards including the Women in Cable Telecommunications (WICT) Board of Directors. She was the Senior Director of Mentoring on the WICT Southeast Chapter Board of Directors when the chapter won the National Award for Excellence in Mentoring in 2011.

You can follow her on LinkedIn, Instagram and Twitter or access new topics for career management on her site, www.careerbluprint.com.

www.ingramcontent.com/pod-product-compliance
Lightning Source LLC
Chambersburg PA
CBHW070959180526
45168CB00003B/1207